BLAZERS

CRIME SOLVERS

GATHERING

BLOOD EVIDENCE

by Melissa Langley Biegert

Consultant:
David Foran, PhD
Director, Forensic Science Program
Michigan State University

Reading Consultant:
Barbara J. Fox
Reading Specialist
North Carolina State University

Capstone

Mankato, Minnesota

Blazers is published by Capstone Press,
151 Good Counsel Drive, P.O. Box 669, Mankato, Minnesota 56002.
www.capstonepress.com

Books published by Capstone Press are manufactured with paper
containing at least 10 percent post-consumer waste.

Library of Congress Cataloging-in-Publication Data
Biegert, Melissa Ann Langley, 1967–
    Gathering blood evidence / by Melissa Langley Biegert.
    p. cm. — (Blazers. Crime solvers)
    Includes bibliographical references and index.
    Summary: "Describes methods used by experts to collect and analyze blood evidence to solve
crimes" — Provided by publisher.
    ISBN 978-1-4296-3373-4 (library binding)
    1. Criminal investigation — Juvenile literature. 2. Evidence, Criminal — Juvenile literature.
3. Blood — Juvenile literature. I. Title. II. Series.
HV8073.8.B52 2010
363.25'62 — dc22
                                                                    2009014606

Editorial Credits

Megan Schoeneberger, editor; Matt Bruning, designer; Eric Gohl, media researcher

Photo Credits

CRIME SOLVERS

GATHERING BLOOD EVIDENCE

TABLE OF CONTENTS

no. 213900192

CHAPTER ONE

THE BLOODSTAIN'S TALE

Detectives search a crime scene.
They find few clues. Then they spot
small drops of blood on the carpet.
These few drops could solve the crime.

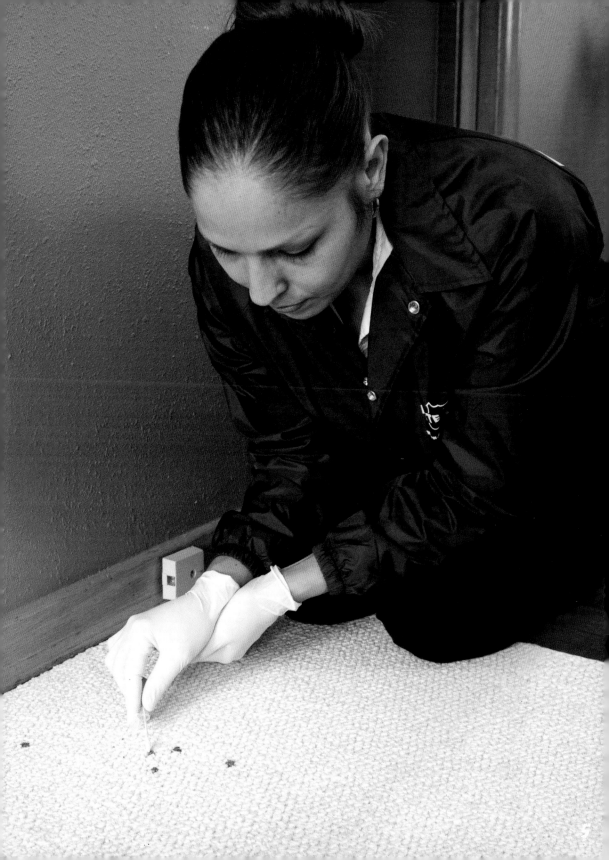

Crime scene experts know that blood drops tell a story. Blood **evidence** can tell who committed a crime. Blood can also show how a crime was committed.

evidence – information, items, and facts that help prove something to be true or false

CHAPTER TWO

ON THE SCENE

Detectives search crime scenes for blood evidence. Sometimes **criminals** try to clean up the blood. But blood is hard to remove. Experts may find blood years after a crime.

criminal – someone who commits a crime

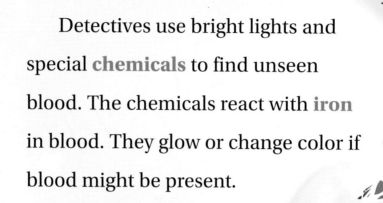

Detectives use bright lights and special **chemicals** to find unseen blood. The chemicals react with **iron** in blood. They glow or change color if blood might be present.

BLAZERS FACT

The chemicals sometimes react with other metals or bleach. More tests are needed to make sure the material is actually blood.

chemical – a substance used in or produced by chemistry

iron – the mineral in blood that carries oxygen to cells

Experts study the shape of blood drops and **spatter**. The size of the drops tells how far and how fast the blood fell. Gunshot wounds leave a spray of small drops. Dripping blood leaves larger drops.

spatter – a pattern of blood drops

Common Blood Spatters

large, dripping blood

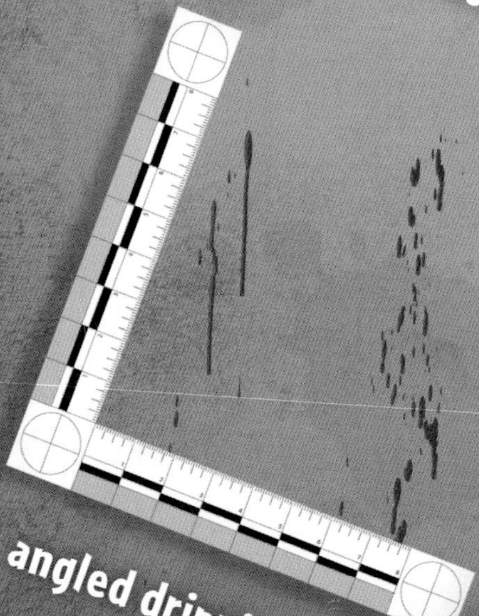

angled dripping blood

high-speed spray

13

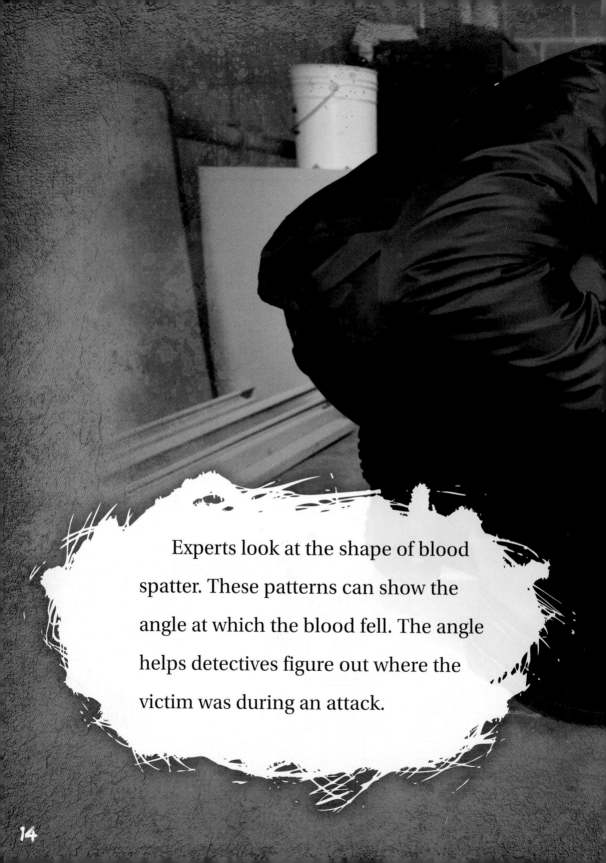

Experts look at the shape of blood spatter. These patterns can show the angle at which the blood fell. The angle helps detectives figure out where the victim was during an attack.

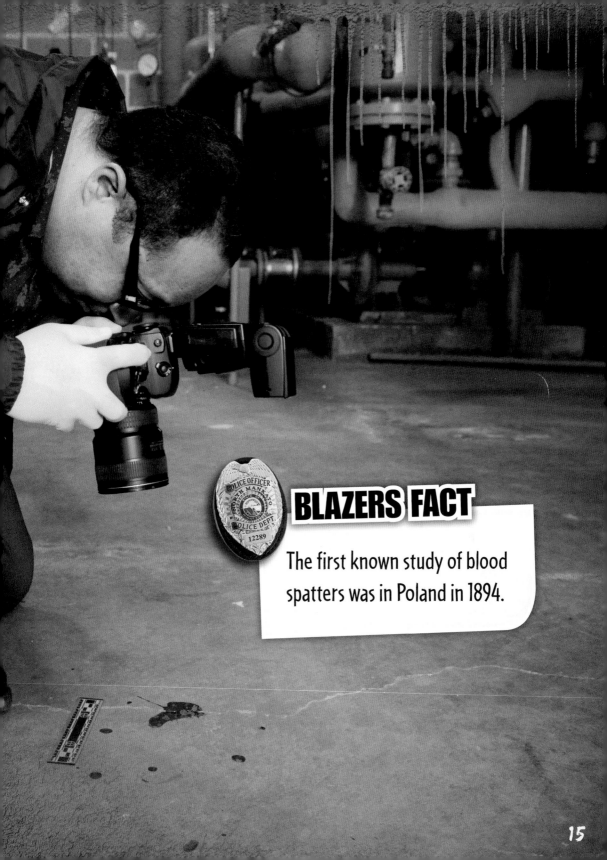

The first known study of blood spatters was in Poland in 1894.

Police look at blood trails to see if victims were moved. Trails may show how they were moved. Smeared blood might mean that someone moved or dragged a victim.

BLAZERS FACT

Blood drops sometimes hold other clues like fingerprints or shoeprints.

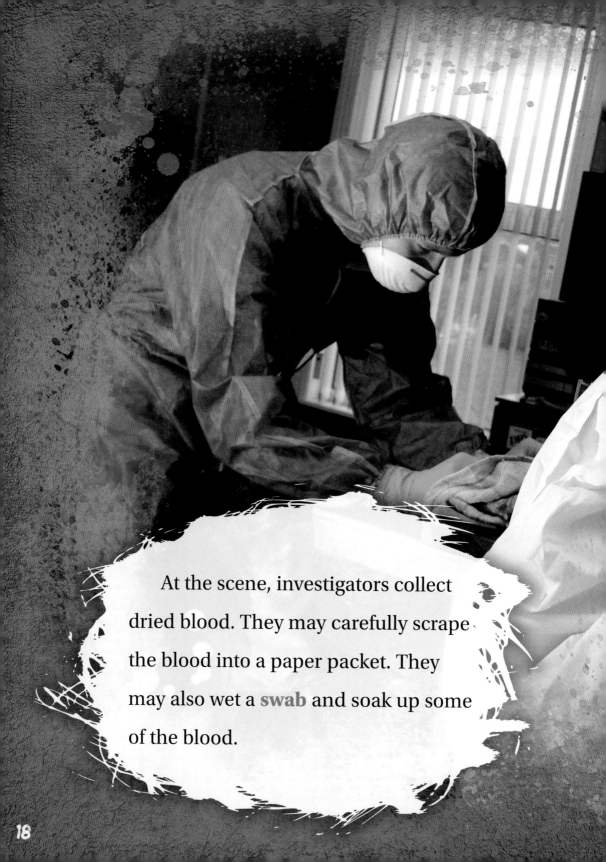

At the scene, investigators collect dried blood. They may carefully scrape the blood into a paper packet. They may also wet a **swab** and soak up some of the blood.

swab – soft material wrapped
around the end of a small stick

CHAPTER THREE

IN THE LAB

Detectives take the samples to a crime lab. Scientists test the samples for human blood.

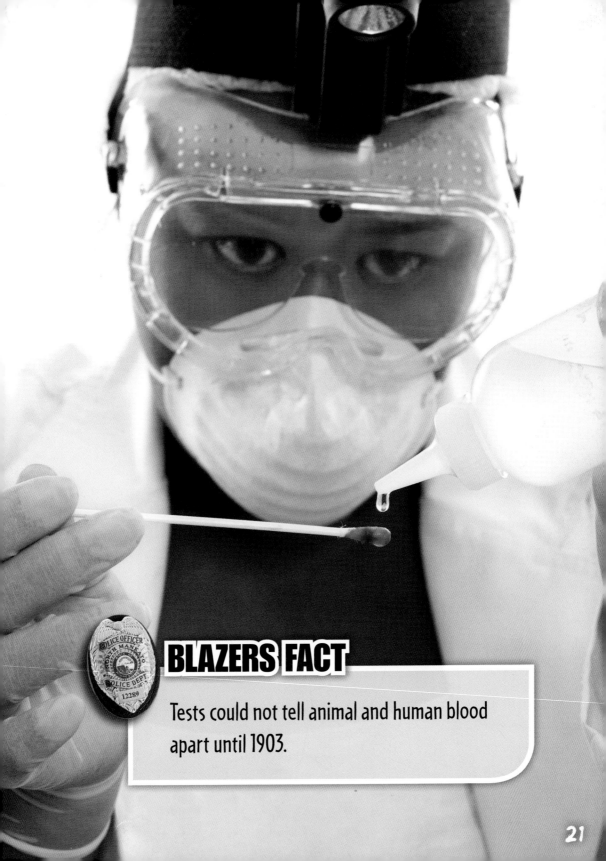

BLAZERS FACT

Tests could not tell animal and human blood apart until 1903.

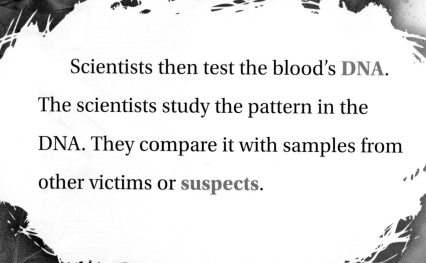

Scientists then test the blood's **DNA**. The scientists study the pattern in the DNA. They compare it with samples from other victims or **suspects**.

BLAZERS FACT

Only identical twins have the same DNA.

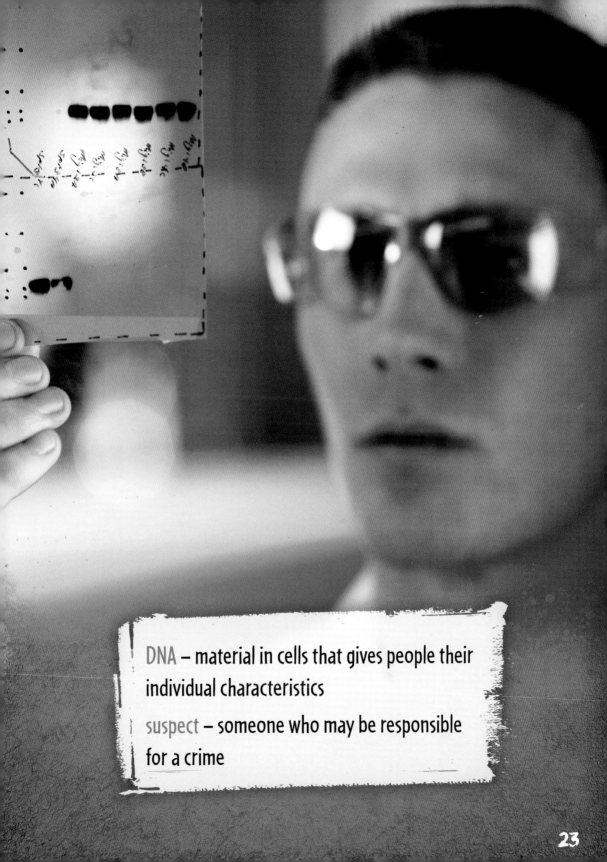

DNA – material in cells that gives people their individual characteristics

suspect – someone who may be responsible for a crime

Sometimes there are no suspects. Experts then compare the DNA to records stored in a **database**. The database contains millions of DNA records.

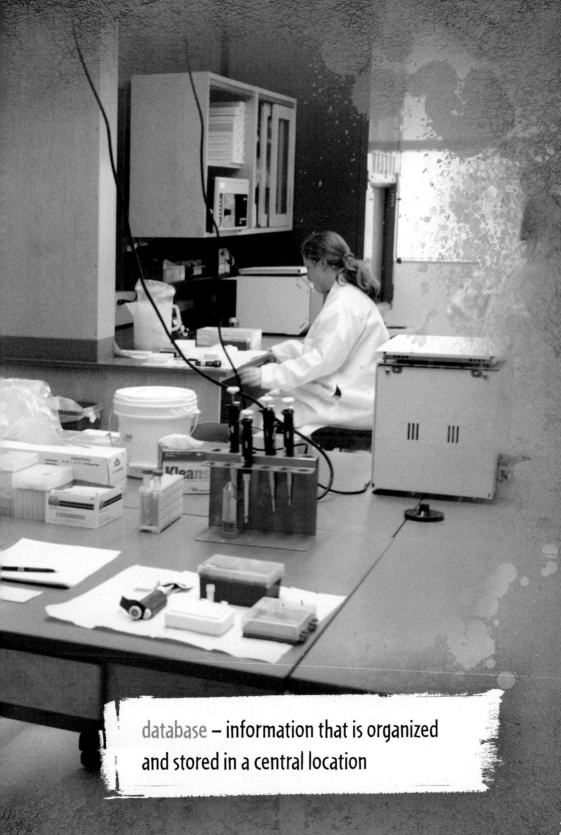

database – information that is organized
and stored in a central location

CHAPTER FOUR

CONNECTING THE DROPS

Blood helps police solve crimes.
It can show what happened during a
crime. Blood can also prove who was
at a crime scene. This information can
put guilty people in jail.

Blood and DNA evidence can also prove someone is innocent. Blood is one of the best clues to help solve crimes.

BLAZERS FACT

In 1869, French police were the first to use blood evidence to solve a major murder case.

Glossary

chemical (KE-muh-kuhl) — a substance used in or produced by chemistry

criminal (KRI-muh-nuhl) — someone who commits a crime

database (DAY-tuh-bays) — information that is organized and stored in a central location

DNA (dee-en-AY) — material in cells that gives people their individual characteristics; DNA stands for deoxyribonucleic acid.

evidence (EV-uh-duhnss) — information, items, and facts that help prove something to be true or false

iron (EYE-urn) — the mineral in blood that carries oxygen to cells

spatter (SPAT-ur) — a pattern of blood drops

suspect (SUHSS-pekt) — someone who may be responsible for a crime

swab (SWAHB) — soft material wrapped around the end of a small stick

Read More

Ballard, Carol. *At the Crime Scene! Collecting Clues and Evidence.* Solve That Crime! Berkeley Heights, N.J.: Enslow, 2009.

Beck, Esther. *Cool Crime Scene Basics: Securing the Scene.* Cool CSI. Edina, Minn.: ABDO, 2009.

Hamilton, Sue. *DNA Analysis: Forensic Fluids and Follicles.* Crime Scene Investigation. Edina, Minn.: ABDO, 2008.

Stille, Darlene R. *Forensic Evidence: Blood.* Crabtree Contact. New York: Crabtree, 2009.

Internet Sites

FactHound offers a safe, fun way to find Internet sites related to this book. All of the sites on FactHound have been researched by our staff.

Here's all you do:

Visit *www.facthound.com*

FactHound will fetch the best sites for you!

Index